Respect!

by

Michaela Morgan

Illustrated by Karen Donnelly

For all the unsung heroes

With thanks to our readers:

Michael Martin

Nick Rees

Hayden Smith

First published 2005 in Great Britain by
Barrington Stoke Ltd
18 Walker Street, Edinburgh, EH3 7LP

www.barringtonstoke.co.uk

This edition published 2011

ISBN: 978-1-84299-989-9

Printed in China by Leo

Contents

Chapter 1
The Children's Home

This is a true story.

The truth.

The whole truth.

And nothing but the truth.

Listen.

It's all about a boy called Tully.

His full name was Walter Tull but his friends called him Tully. So that's what we'll call him.

He was 7 when his mum died. It wasn't very long before his dad married again. His new step-mum and her kids came to live in Tully's house. There wasn't much room.

Then 2 years later, his dad died too.

So at 9 years old Tully was an orphan.

His step-mum kept her own kids at home with her but Tully and Eddie, his 4-year-old brother, were taken away from their real house by the sea and sent off to a Children's Home.

The Children's Home was in the East End of London – far away from where Tully had grown up. He didn't have any friends in London. Not one. All Tully had was his little brother Eddie.

It was hard to get used to the sounds and the smells of a town like London. And some of the other kids were mean.

Tully and Eddie looked different. They came to the Home in old clothes – they were just rags really. Some of the bigger kids made fun of them. One of the biggest kids was Harry.

Harry took every chance to make life hard for the new kids. He was a bully.

Other kids stayed away from Tully and Eddie – they didn't want to get on the wrong side of Harry.

One day someone sent a box of apples into the Home. "So what!" you're thinking. "Apples! Big deal!" But it was a big deal to the kids in the Home. It was a very big deal.

The kids were told they could have just one apple each and the big kids (Harry's gang) could have the extra "windfalls".

Little Eddie picked his apple. "What's a windfall?" he asked. Eddie was still only 4 and Tully had to explain lots of things to him.

"A windfall is an apple that's fallen to the ground," Tully told him.

"So if an apple falls to the ground, it's mine!" said Harry and he stuck out his long leg and tripped little Eddie up.

The small boy went flying and so did the apple. Up into the air it went and Harry

waited for it to fall to the ground so he could have it.

But the apple never landed on the ground.

Tully stuck his foot out and the apple landed on his toe. Then he flicked it to his knee and passed it from knee to knee, foot to foot, on to his head, on to his back and then on to his head again. Harry made a grab for it but Tully was too quick for him. Tully was brilliant at this game of Keepy Uppy. He could do it for ages.

All the other kids came round to watch.

They were clapping and slapping Tully on the back. "Show us how to do that!" they said.

That was how Eddie got his apple. And that was how Tully got the respect of all the other kids.

He and Eddie had friends now and Harry gave up picking on them. Sorted!

The Home was run by the church. The staff made sure the kids knew right from wrong. The staff fed the kids and gave them clothes to wear. They sent the kids to school and they trained them to work. But they didn't look after the kids like a real mum and dad.

It was Tully who looked after little Eddie. It can't have been easy for him. There was no-one to look after *HIM*. And Tully was only 9 years old.

He had known a life with a mum and a dad to look after him. He had lived in a family house, by the sea, and now here he was in the East End of London where he knew no-one.

And now he had a little brother he had to look after.

He had to grow up fast!

"Oh!" I bet you're saying to yourself, "Where were the Social Workers? Where were the foster parents?" And so on. Well, let me tell you – the year was 1897. Yes – 1897! A long, long time ago. Are you amazed to hear that?

And here's another thing you should know – Tully and Eddie were the only two black boys in a Children's Home full of white kids – and things were very different back then.

Here are some of the things that were different for Tully and his friends.

They had no TV.

No radios.

They had no phones.

No mobiles.

They had no computers.

No fridges.

No hot showers and baths.

No proper heating.

The kids were often very cold. They were nearly always hungry.

Here's some of the things they DID have. They had:

Horses clip-clopping on the cobble-stones.

Gas lamps on the streets.

Kids dying of hunger and disease.

And teachers who beat them with belts.

Some things were the same.

The boys were all mad about football.

They played in the streets. The kids could get up a footie team in no time at all. Tully was their star.

Chapter 2
Football

Tully was always kicking a ball.

If he didn't have a ball, he kicked stones.
If he didn't have stones, he kicked bits of
rag. Or tins. Or boxes. Or anything! And
boy could he hit the ball! He could dribble.
He could pass. He could tackle. And he
could score.

The kids made up a Children's Home team and he was their star player. They always made him Captain and everyone wanted to be on his team.

He was a good Captain. He had brilliant football skills and he was a brilliant leader too. He was fair. He didn't lose his temper. All the kids respected him.

And boy he could play!

Oh, you talk of your stars now. You talk of David Beckham or Wayne Rooney or Frank Lampard or Theo Walcott, but Tully was as good as the best of them. Tully was better than the best.

The kids in the Home knew he was good, but one day they knew for sure. He was spotted by a scout for a local team.

It was an amateur team. They were called Clapton FC and they were the best team in the area. When Clapton picked Tully to play for them, the other kids in his

Children's Home team were as proud as proud can be. They went on and on about it to everyone – to anyone – who would listen. They told all the other kids they met. They told all the other kids at the Children's Home (of course). They told everyone at school. They told the baker, the coalman. They told passers-by. They showed off to anyone who would listen.

Tully didn't go round shouting about it. He was never the type to show off. But he had plenty he *could* have shown off about.

Clapton FC was an amateur team but they were the best. The very best. With Tully playing for them they won everything. Walter Tull had become a famous name.

They won the FA Amateur Cup – the top prize in amateur football. And they won it 6-0!

They won everything. They won the London Senior Cup. And they won the London County Amateur Club cup. They really were the best.

When Tully was picked to play for them he was called "the catch of the season".

But this was only the start.

He was soon spotted again. This time by a professional team. Tottenham Hotspurs – yes the Spurs! Walter Tull, or Tully to the kids, played for Spurs.

Chapter 3
Star!

Tully was the very first black out-field player in professional football. A star!

Of course plenty of people had a go at him but Tully just stood strong. He would never pick fights.

Bit by bit everyone – the other Spurs players and the Spurs fans – came to like and admire this strong, proud man. He earned their respect.

Tully's very first match for Spurs was in 1909. It was Spurs first game after they went up to the top division. Tully ran onto that field and he played like a dream. He played in front of a crowd of 30,000 cheering fans.

He was brilliant. Everyone said so. He could pass the ball 35 yards right to the winger's feet. The newspapers all said he was the star of the team. His future was bright. Very bright. But later that year something happened.

He was playing at an away match at Bristol City when it started.

Every time the ball went near him, the Bristol crowd started to yell at him. They couldn't have a go at him for his playing – so they got at him because he was black.

"Get back to your jungle, darkie!" they shouted.

They made up rude songs about him. They spat at him. Every time he got the ball, they made monkey noises.

There he was standing in the middle of that huge football ground – the only black face in a sea of white. All around him people hissed and spat and shouted.

It must have seemed like a nightmare. This had never happened before in football. It shocked Tully. It shocked the rest of the team too. It even shocked the newspaper reporters.

"They're just a bunch of fools and idiots!" said one of Tully's team-mates. "Don't let them get to you."

"Who do they think they are to pick on you!" said another mate. "You're ten times better than they could ever dream of being."

"Just a bunch of fools," the team agreed.

"Don't let them get to you!"

Chapter 4
A New Start

Tully put his faith in fairness, hard work and kindness. He always stood up strong and proud, but what happened at Bristol *did* get to him. He felt sick about it.

He almost lost his nerve. He didn't play much for the rest of the season.

He spoke about it a lot. He thought about it a lot. He went over and over it but he couldn't get to grips with it. It's hard to come to terms with something so unfair. But there is a saying: "What doesn't kill you, makes you stronger." Tully pulled himself together bit by bit and made a new start.

The next season he took a transfer to another team. He went to Northampton Town. They were a BIG team back then. Things change! Northampton paid a very big transfer fee for him.

He soon became the star of his new team. He played 110 games and was their most popular player.

His little brother Eddie was proud of him. But, by this time, Eddie was living far away.

He had been adopted. The family who adopted him lived in Scotland. So that's where he was – up in Scotland – far, far from Northampton and his famous brother.

They kept in touch. They wrote letters. They sent cards. Tully sent Eddie bits from the newspaper all about his success.

The years passed 1910 ... 1911 ... 1912 ... 1913. Tully and Eddie missed each other. Then in 1914 Tully had the chance of a transfer to Rangers.

Glasgow Rangers – just around the corner from his little brother!

Both Tully and Eddie were over the moon at the idea of living near each other again and Rangers were over the moon to have the chance of having Walter Tull to play for them. He was the best! Everything was going to be *brilliant*.

Then in the summer of 1914 war broke out.

Chapter 5
War

It was 1914 and Tully was now known as Private Walter Tull. He was just a plain soldier. He had been one of the first to sign up to fight for his country in the First World War.

He didn't know much about war. But he soon found out.

The first thing he learnt was how to march. Then he was marched off into the middle of nowhere. He started in France.

The men lived in muddy freezing trenches in the ground.

In the trenches it was cold. It was wet. It was boring. It was alive with rats and fleas. And it was muddy.

You spent your time lying in mud, sleeping in mud, soaked in mud. Some men even drowned in mud.

And when you popped your head up out of the trench – you got shot at.

Men were killed every day.

Tully went to the Somme. The worst battle of the war and he was in it.

Back at home, Eddie read about it in the newspapers and in Tully's letters and later,

much later he read about it in the history
books. And still Eddie found it hard to
believe.

Hard to imagine.

You try it.

On one morning in the battle of the
Somme this is what happened.

Nearly 20,000 (twenty thousand!) British
men were killed.

Over 35,000 (Yes that's right – thirty-five thousand) were wounded.

585 were captured alive. Many were just listed as "missing". This could mean they were found shot and no-one knew who they were. Or they were blown up into small pieces. Or they simply sunk into holes in the mud.

In all, nearly 60,000 men were killed, wounded or lost – in just one morning.

That's the same number of men as two sell-out crowds at Spurs home ground.

Think of it.

Sixty thousand men lost and what did they win? They won a few yards of mud.

Chapter 6
Wounded

There has never been a battle like it. Never. And Tully was there. He survived it. He survived a nightmare of blood and mud, guns crashing, men screaming, friends dying. Not only did he survive – he did well. He kept a cool head. He looked after all those around him. He became a leader.

The officers praised him for keeping his cool. They said he was one of the bravest men they had ever met. In a report they said he should have a medal.

He was in other battles, too. In France and in Italy he fought on until he was wounded and sent off to hospital.

Now in those days – and still today – there was a huge difference between officers and plain soldiers. Officers had been to posh schools, and were often rich. "Men", or plain soldiers, didn't get the chance to become officers and in those days black men were just not *allowed* to become officers. There was an army law against it.

But they changed that law for Walter Tull.

So when he left the hospital and went back to the battle field, he went back as an officer. Walter Tull, Eddie's brother, Tully, was the first ever British born black officer in the British army.

It's true. You can look it up in the history books. He, the grandson of a slave, a poor orphan, who had to make his own way in the world, became the first black man to lead white men into battle.

Chapter 7
1918

Tully was posted back to France for another battle in the Somme.

It was the year of 1918. This was the year that the war ended but just before the end of the war Walter Tull was shot.

It was one of the final battles of the war. Walter and his men had been ordered to leave their trench and go "over the top" towards the enemy.

Over the top they went. Shells crashed around them, bullets rained down on them. Then suddenly, Tully was on the ground. He had been shot.

He fell into the mud in the middle of the battle field, between the British and the German lines. They called this place "No

Man's Land". There was very little chance of saving anyone who fell here.

But to the men, Tully was not just an officer. He was a real friend.

They ran to his rescue. They ran through a hail of bullets. They ran through exploding shells but they couldn't get to him.

They tried again. And again. And again. They tried their best but they couldn't save him. Tully died.

Eddie learnt of all this in a letter sent to him by the Officer in Charge. The officer said Walter Tull had been one of the bravest and most popular men he'd ever met. "The army has lost a faithful officer", he wrote "and we have lost a friend".

Tully was awarded the British War Medal and the Victory Medal and was recommended for a Military Cross. Here they are.

Chapter 8
The End

So that's how the grandson of a slave, an orphan dressed in rags, grew to become the first black British army officer.

He fought in the Somme and survived to fight there again. Not many soldiers could say that.

He won medals in the war and he won the cup in football. He played for the best teams in the country.

He looked after his team-mates on the football field. He looked after his men on the battle field – and he looked after his little brother after his parents had died.

He was a strong, proud man.

A hero.

This story is true. Parts of it may be hard to imagine. Parts of it may be hard to believe – but it is the truth. The whole truth and nothing but the truth.

It was so long ago now, most people have forgotten about Walter Tull.

What would he think about the world we live in now? What would he think about the things that have changed and the things that have stayed the same? What would he say if he could talk to us?

And what would you say if you met him now? I bet I know what you'd say.

"Respect!"

A Note from the Author

One day I was leafing through a newspaper when I found a report of a new exhibition in Manchester. In it there were a few lines about the life of Walter Tull. I was amazed! He had done so much! He was such a hero! And yet I had never heard of him before.

I asked everyone I met, "Have you ever heard of Walter Tull?" Nobody had. He was almost completely unknown.

I thought Walter Tull deserved to be famous. His story needed to be told. So I've done my best to tell it here. It's all true – and if you don't believe me you can check it out on the Internet!